THE GREEKS

AGAMEMNON TO ALEXANDER THE GREAT

TERENCE CLARK

CANADIAN MUSEUM OF HISTORY
MUSÉE CANADIEN DE L'HISTOIRE

Library and Archives Canada
Cataloguing in Publication

Clark, Terence
The Greeks – Agamemnon to Alexander
the Great / Terence Clark.

(Souvenir catalogue series)
Issued also in French under title:
Les Grecs – D'Agamemnon à Alexandre le Grand.
ISBN 978-0-660-20308-9
Cat. no.: NM23-5/10-2014E

1. Greece – Antiquities – Exhibitions.
2. Classical antiquities – Exhibitions.
3. Greece – History – Exhibitions.
4. Greece – Civilization – Exhibitions.

I.   Canadian Museum of History.
II. Title.
III. Series: Souvenir catalogue series.

DF11.3 G38 C53 2014
949.500909074
C2014-980050-9

Published by the
Canadian Museum of History
100 Laurier Street
Gatineau, QC K1A 0M8
www.historymuseum.ca

Souvenir Catalogue series, 10
ISSN 2291-6385

This work is a souvenir of the exhibition **The Greeks – Agamemnon to Alexander the Great**, which was developed by the Hellenic Ministry of Culture and Sports (Athens, Greece), the Canadian Museum of History (Gatineau, Canada), the National Geographic Museum (Washington, DC, USA), The Field Museum (Chicago, USA), and Pointe-à-Callière, Montréal Archaeology and History Complex (Montréal, Canada).

Table of Contents

Foreword

Almost every aspect of our lives today bears the imprint of ancient Greece. Politics and philosophy, literature and the arts, mathematics and medicine, architecture and sports — all have been influenced by traditions developed or perfected in ancient Greece. **The Greeks – Agamemnon to Alexander the Great** provides an extraordinary and captivating insight into how the "cradle of Western civilization" came to be, how it changed the world and how it endures today in the hearts and minds of the Greek people.

The exhibition is remarkable in its size, scope and splendour. It is the most comprehensive exhibition about ancient Greek history to ever tour outside of Greece, spanning over 5,000 years of history and featuring over 500 exquisite artifacts, including some of the finest treasures of antiquity. It animates that history through the compelling stories of individuals great and small, mythical and historical.

The Greeks – Agamemnon to Alexander the Great is presented to enhance our collective understanding and appreciation of Greek history and culture, and the Greek people's prodigious contributions to humanity. Tour the exhibition and encounter dazzling jewellery from the royal tombs of Mycenae, magnificent sculptures of the Archaic period and the Golden Age of Greece, and ancient artifacts that will take you back to the first Olympics and the very birth of democracy. Meet Greek philosophers and epic poets, as well as gods of Greek mythology, such as Aristotle, Plato and Homer; Aphrodite, Zeus and Poseidon.

Our museums are proud to have worked together to bring these treasures and stories to North America, something none of us could have accomplished on our own. Our consortium was organized and led by the Canadian Museum of History. The Museum also led our joint production of the exhibition in association with the Directorate General of Antiquities and Cultural Heritage of the Hellenic Ministry of Culture, Education and Religious Affairs, whose partnership was instrumental to the project's success.

We extend special thanks to Greece's Minister of Culture, Konstantinos Tassoulas; Lina Mendoni, General Secretary of Culture; and Maria Vlazaki-Andreadaki, Director General of the Directorate of Antiquities and Cultural Heritage and her team. Their collective vision, passion and hard work on the project's behalf were nothing short of inspirational. We also extend our sincere thanks to the 21 Greek museums that generously provided artifacts for the exhibition and assistance to our curators.

Pericles, the prominent statesman and orator from the Golden Age of Greece, is often paraphrased for saying that what humans leave behind is not what is engraved in stone monuments but rather what is woven into the lives of others. It would be hard to overstate the influence of ancient Greece on the lives of all who have followed. We are all inheritors of this incredible legacy. In that sense, **The Greeks – Agamemnon to Alexander the Great** is not just about them, it's also about us.

Mark O'Neill
President and Chief Executive Officer
Canadian Museum of History
Gatineau, Canada

Francine Lelièvre
Executive Director, Pointe-à-Callière
Montréal Archaeology and History Complex
Montréal, Canada

Gary Knell
President and Chief Executive Officer
National Geographic Society
Washington, DC, USA

Richard W. Lariviere
President and Chief Executive Officer
The Field Museum
Chicago, USA

The Travelling Exhibition

December 12, 2014 – April 26, 2015
Pointe-à-Callière, Montréal Archaeology
and History Complex
Montréal, Canada

November 24, 2015 – April 10, 2016
The Field Museum
Chicago, USA

 CANADIAN MUSEUM OF HISTORY
MUSÉE CANADIEN DE L'HISTOIRE

 NATIONAL
GEOGRAPHIC

June 5 – October 12, 2015
Canadian Museum of History
Gatineau, Canada

June 1 – October 10, 2016
National Geographic Museum
Washington, DC, USA

Free App

Delve deeper into the world of the Greeks with the free mobile app. Simply
hold your smart phone or tablet over certain pages of the souvenir catalogue
to trigger enhanced content: videos, interactive maps, games and more!

From Neolithic beginnings to the death of Alexander the Great, **The Greeks** presents the milestones of more than 5,000 years of Greek history and culture through the perspective of individuals, revealing how they viewed themselves and the world around them, in life and in death.

Dimini Amulet
Steatite
Dimini, 4800–3300 BCE

This small stone amulet may show a
person in reverent repose, crouched
beneath the awesome power of the
supernatural. It may also depict a dead
body, and may have acted as an amulet
to protect against an untimely death.

The Aegean Prelude

6,500 to 1,450 BCE

In this early period, communities
began to take shape on the Greek
mainland, as well as on islands
throughout the Aegean Sea.
Technologies developed, goods were
exchanged, and rituals appeared —
setting the stage for the appearance,
during the Bronze Age, of a Minoan
elite and the construction of their
palaces on Crete.

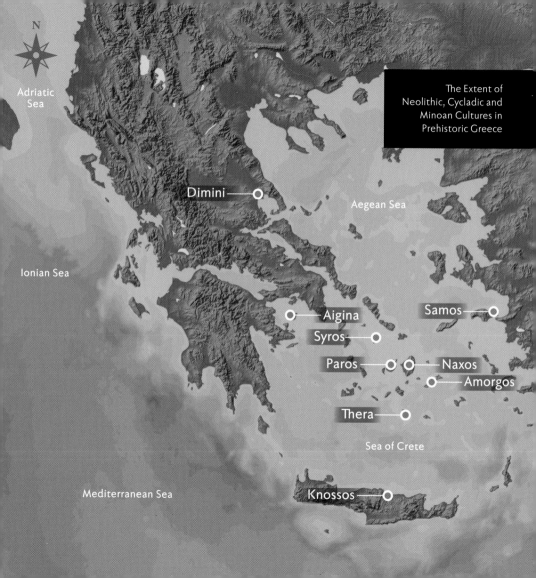

N

Adriatic
Sea

Ionian Sea

Dimini

Aegean Sea

The Extent of
Neolithic, Cycladic and
Minoan Cultures in
Prehistoric Greece

Samos

Aigina

Syros

Paros   Naxos

Amorgos

Thera

Sea of Crete

Mediterranean Sea

Knossos

The Neolithic Period

The Neolithic peoples of the Aegean were hunter-gatherers who moved seasonally in order to survive. In time, they began to work the land, raise livestock, and establish villages. They also amassed surplus food and other products, which they traded for foreign goods.

With the dawn of the Neolithic Period, people became preoccupied with fertility, both human and agricultural. Figurines symbolizing reproduction through the female form, with emphasized breasts, belly and pubic area, became widespread. They were likely used in fertility and initiation rites.

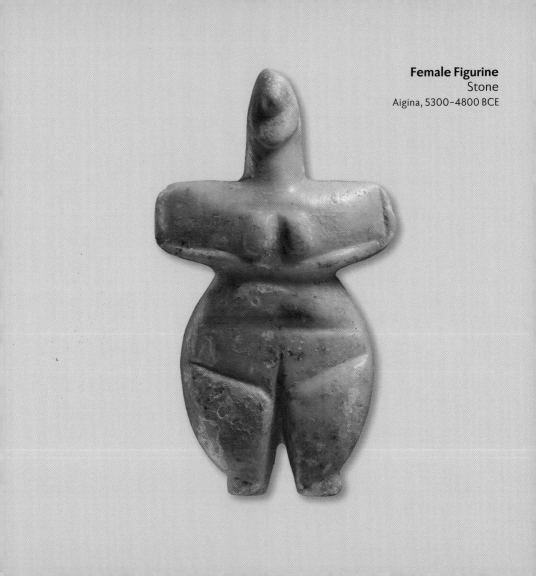

Female Figurine
Stone
Aigina, 5300–4800 BCE

Cycladic Culture

Around 3200 BCE, a thriving culture emerged in the Cyclades, a circle of islands at the heart of the Aegean Sea. This location was ideal for the exchange of goods and ideas: boats could travel to and from mainland Greece, Crete and Asia Minor.

Control of these maritime trade routes, coupled with the quality of goods produced by local artisans, led to the rise of a wealthy upper class in the Cyclades.

"Frying Pan"
Clay
Syros, 2800–2300 BCE

"Frying Pan"

Objects like this have been found in tombs and the remains of dwellings. Archaeologists refer to them as "frying pans," but their purpose is unclear. Theories of their function abound: were they perhaps serving platters? Given the raised rim, could they have been filled with water and used as mirrors? Or even to detect earthquakes when ripples disturbed the water's surface?

The exterior of this vessel depicts an oared longboat being rowed across the swirling pattern of waves. Boats such as this were used for trade and communication on the Aegean Sea.

Cycladic Figurines

Cycladic figurines, often found in tombs, are among the most iconic artifacts in Greek archaeology. Traces of pigment on one of the figurines seen here suggest that it once had painted eyes. Another was deliberately broken, like others found in the same grave, suggesting a funerary ritual that has yet to be understood. They were probably used for ritual purposes or as offerings to the deceased.

"Violin-Shaped"
Female Figurine
Marble
Paros, 3200–2800 BCE

Female Figurine
Marble
Amorgos, 2800–2300 BCE

Female Figurine
Marble
Naxos, 2800–2300 BCE

**Male Figurine Performing
the "Minoan Salute"**
Bronze
Tylissos, 1600–1450 BCE

Goddess with Upraised Arms
Clay
Knossos, 1375–1200 BCE

The Minoan World

The first "European" civilization
appeared on the island of Crete around
2700 BCE. Communities sprang up
around palaces, which served as seats
of political and administrative power.

Minoan culture was spectacular, as
suggested by the ruins of the most
important of these palaces, Knossos.
Supported by a powerful elite, art and
writing flourished, and Minoan culture
would have a lasting impact on
Greek civilization.

Eruption of Thera (17th Century BCE)

Starting with the massive eruption of Thera — an event that obliterated much of the island now known as Santorini — the Minoan world began to crumble. One of the largest known volcanic eruptions in history, it changed global weather patterns, and may also have inspired stories of the mythical lost continent of Atlantis.

Exodus Across the Aegean Sea as Thera's Volcano Erupts

Labrys (Double Axe)
Bronze
Arkalochori cave,
around 1700–1600 BCE

Theseus and the Minotaur

The double axe was an important Minoan symbol of power and ritual. It was used to sacrifice bulls to the gods. The name for the axe, *labrys*, comes from the ancient Greek word for "labyrinth." It recalls the myth of Theseus and the Minotaur.

In legend, King Minos refused to sacrifice a particularly beautiful bull to Poseidon, god of the sea. Instead Minos kept the bull for himself and sacrificed a lesser animal to the god.

As punishment, the gods cursed the king's wife to fall in love with the beautiful bull. This cursed love begat the Minotaur, a monster with the body of a man and the head of a bull, which fed on human flesh. King Minos built the famed labyrinth to house the monster and offered young men and women to the Minotaur as sacrificial meals. The hero, Theseus, used his wit and courage to slay the fearsome beast and end the curse.

Rulers and Warriors of the Mycenaean World

16th to 12th Centuries BCE

Around the middle of the Bronze Age (1600 BCE), the Mycenaean civilization developed in the southern regions of mainland Greece. Unlike the Minoans before them, who focused much of their attention on art and trade, the Mycenaeans had a penchant for war. Mycenaean communities established a hierarchical system led by a king, or *wanax*, and administered by a series of bureaucrats.

The Discovery of Mycenae

After successfully finding the ruins of the city of Troy, in Turkey, in the 1870s, archaeologist Heinrich Schliemann turned his attention to the other main city mentioned in Homer's *Iliad*, Mycenae, and its mythical king, Agamemnon.

Wary of dubious excavation techniques and keen to hold on to the treasures recovered from Mycenae, the Greek Archaeological Society assigned Panagiotis Stamatakis to oversee Schliemann's project and protect Greece's cultural heritage.

The two men uncovered lavish riches of the kings and queens of Mycenae from Grave Circle A, within the citadel's walls. While Schliemann thought he had found Agamemnon, we know now that these graves are 300 years older than the Trojan War and could not possibly be those of Agamemnon and his family.

Schliemann at the Famed Lion Gate, Entrance to Mycenae in the 1870s

"I have gazed upon the eyes of Agamemnon."

Schliemann uttered these words when he first saw this golden death mask in Grave V. Associating this discovery with the Greek hero, he believed that nearby remains were those of the wife and companions of the mythical conqueror of Troy.

It was placed over the face of a mummified person who died in his or her thirties. This mask has never before left Greece.

Funerary Mask
Gold
Mycenae, Circle A, Grave V,
second half of the 16th century BCE

The "Mask of Agamemnon"
Gold
Second half of the 16th century BCE

Also in Grave V was this breathtaking gold mask of a bearded man. Its beauty and detail convinced Schliemann to change his mind and attribute this one to Agamemnon. Since then, it has been known as the "Mask of Agamemnon," one of the most celebrated symbols of Greek archaeology.

Grave V – A Royal Grave

Double-Eagle Necklace
Gold
Mycenae, Circle A, Grave V,
second half of the 16th century BCE

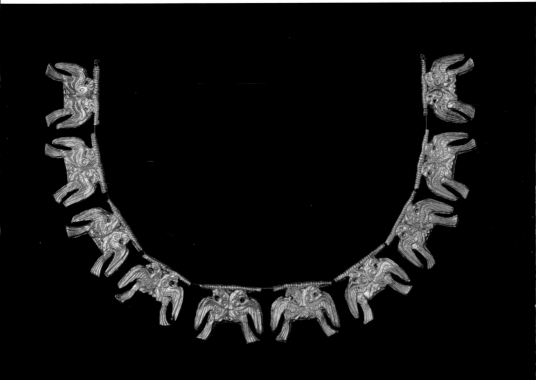

Dagger
Bronze, gold, niello
Mycenae, Circle A, Grave V,
second half of the 16th century BCE

Double-Eagle Necklace

The warrior buried in Grave V was
wearing this opulent necklace. Each
pendant features a double-faced
eagle. This powerful bird of prey was
also depicted on the weapons of
Mycenaean nobles.

Dagger

The triangular blade of this dagger
is a masterpiece of Mycenaean
craftsmanship. From base to tip,
the spiral decoration has been
perfectly scaled to the blade's
narrowing surface.

Grave III – The Grave of the Priestess

Hundreds of gold ornaments were found in a woman's grave, the most luxurious burial of all in Grave Circle A. Five ornaments bore an image of the tripartite shrine, a temple that provides an important clue to the woman's role when she was alive. Likely a priestess, she would have prayed to the gods on behalf of common Mycenaeans. The other golden symbols present in the grave underscore the ritual power of this woman.

These objects would have been sewn onto a beautiful garment of colourful linen or wool.

Cutout Plaque
Gold
Mycenae, Circle A, Grave III,
second half of the 16th century BCE

Tripartite Shrine Appliqué
Gold
Mycenae, Circle A, Grave III,
second half of the 16th century BCE

Roundels
Gold
Mycenae, Circle A, Grave III,
second half of the 16th century BCE

Grave IV

Three men and two women were buried in Grave IV. They may have been members of the same family. When the last person — perhaps a prince — was buried, earlier grave goods were pushed aside to make room for his own. Among the offerings were several ceremonial vessels.

Rhyton (Ceremonial Cup)
White alabaster
Mycenae, Circle A, Grave IV,
second half of the 16th century BCE

Rhyton (Ceremonial Cup)

Equipped with three detachable handles, this remarkably elegant ritual vessel was used to offer libations to the gods. The user either poured liquid onto the ground from the quatrefoil lip, or let it flow through a small hole in the bottom. Fragile and hard to handle, it was probably not used often. The exceptional skill of the artisan, who sculpted it from a single block of stone, as well as its design, indicates a Minoan origin.

Octopus-Shaped Cutout
Gold
Mycenae, Circle A, Grave IV,
second half of the 16th century BCE

Octopus-Shaped Cutouts

Small gold octopi like these — 53 in all — were found in the grave. Each has seven tentacles, rather than the usual eight. A giant octopus, *Haliphron atlanticus*, the eighth tentacle of which is visible only during reproduction, may have frequented the Mediterranean in ancient times. Some Mycenaean palaces were also embellished with octopus imagery. Could this swift-moving, intelligent predator have been the symbol of Mycenae?

Cup
Gold
Mycenae, Circle A, Grave VI,
second half of the 16th century BCE

Grave VI – Stamatakis Alone

Schliemann was convinced he was unearthing the graves of Agamemnon and his family. When he found five graves, the number he was expecting according to the *Iliad*, he concluded his excavation and left Mycenae. Stamatakis continued alone and found a sixth grave within Grave Circle A. Though lacking the same type of opulent riches found in the other graves, Grave VI was more professionally excavated and better documented.

It contained the remains of two men, along with many grave goods. One of the men had died in his twenties; the other, a kinsman, died around the age of thirty.

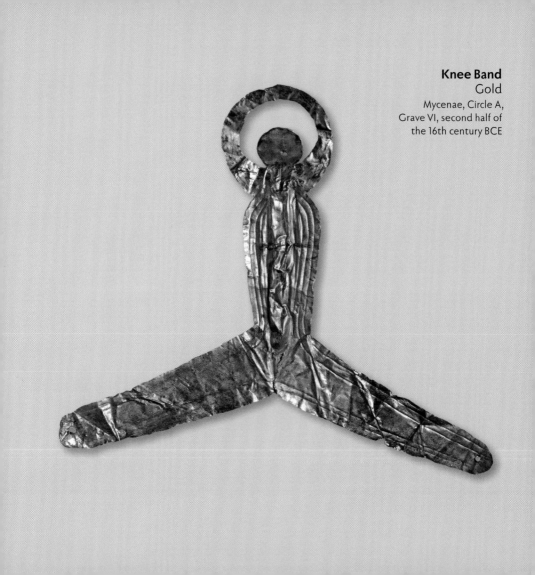

Knee Band
Gold
Mycenae, Circle A,
Grave VI, second half of
the 16th century BCE

Appealing to the Gods

Mycenaean figurines have often been found in the remains of shrines and palaces. Their upturned arms suggest an act of prayer.

Female Figurines
Clay
Tiryns, 1190–1130 BCE

Mycenaean Seals

For powerful Mycenaean nobles, pressing an engraved seal or ring into fresh clay was the equivalent of a signature. Personal motifs were superbly rendered in miniature for all time.

"Mistress of the Animals" Seal

On this seal (top left), a woman is flanked by two lions rearing up on their hind legs. Above her is a sacred motif: two snakes looking at a double axe. This seal may have been part of a necklace used by a priestess who personified a goddess while in a trance.

Seal Rings

In the religious ceremony depicted on this ring (top right), the central figure is a deity. On the left, a man shakes a tree: the dwelling place of the gods. On the right, a woman leans on an altar, resting her head on her arms in a state of "sacred slumber."

This ring depicts a man with a branch in his hand (bottom left), approaching a building with a small tree above it. Behind him stands a goat, probably intended for sacrifice.

Two female figures with raised arms pray by a shrine or altar (bottom right). The branches on either side of the central structure may indicate that the ritual is related to seasonal cycles and fertility.

"Mistress of the Animals" Seal
Carnelian
Mycenae, end of the 15th century BCE

Seal Rings
Gold
Mycenae, around 1500 BCE

Boar-Tusk Helmet
Wild boar tusks
Spata, 13th century BCE

A Warrior's Helmet

Mycenaean warriors wore helmets made of the tusks of dozens of wild boars — which they first had to hunt and kill. The helmets demonstrated the courage and strength of those who wore them. Only the Mycenaeans chose this means of expressing their identity and the value they placed on courage. Many of these helmets, worn in battle, have survived.

**Furniture Inlay Depicting
a Mycenaean Warrior**
Hippopotamus ivory
Mycenae, 14th to 13th centuries BCE

Ancient Greek Deciphered

Numerous clay tablets were baked in fire, allowing them to be preserved for all time. For 3,000 years, the symbols that the Mycenaeans carved into the wet clay remained a secret. It was not until 1953 that their script, Linear B, was deciphered, and the words of the Mycenaeans could be read once again.

Written in an early form of ancient Greek, the tablets often reveal precise inventories of land, taxes, and goods. Some of them also bear the names of Greek gods and goddesses, including Zeus, Hera and Poseidon.

Linear B Tablets
Clay
Pylos, end of the 13th century BCE

Heroes of the Iron Age

11th to 8th Centuries BCE

The most magnificent palaces of the Mycenaean world and the written script they used were abandoned. The peoples and culture persisted and even flourished with the development of iron working technology.

The memories of glorious Bronze Age heroes were remembered and shared as oral history. Later enshrined in the writings of the great Greek poet Homer, the exploits of these heroes would inspire warriors and artisans of the Iron Age.

The Journey
of Odysseus

Island of Circe

The Sirens

Land of the Laestrygonians

Troy

Land of the Cyclops

Ithaca

Poseidon

Homer's Epics –
Myth and History

Homer, the greatest epic poet of ancient Greece, probably lived during the 8th century BCE. Little is known of the poet himself. But he recorded the oral histories of gods and heroes that have captured literary imaginations ever since. His *Iliad* and *Odyssey* mark the beginning of Western literature.

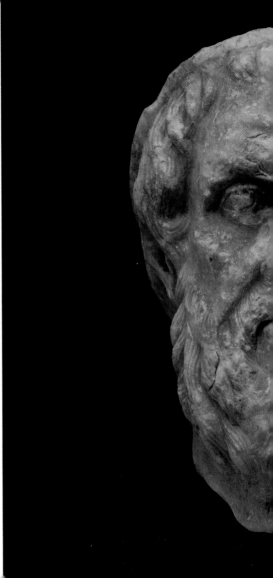

Portrait of Homer
Pentelic marble
Provenance unknown,
mid-2nd century CE
(Roman copy of a Greek
original from about 300 BCE)

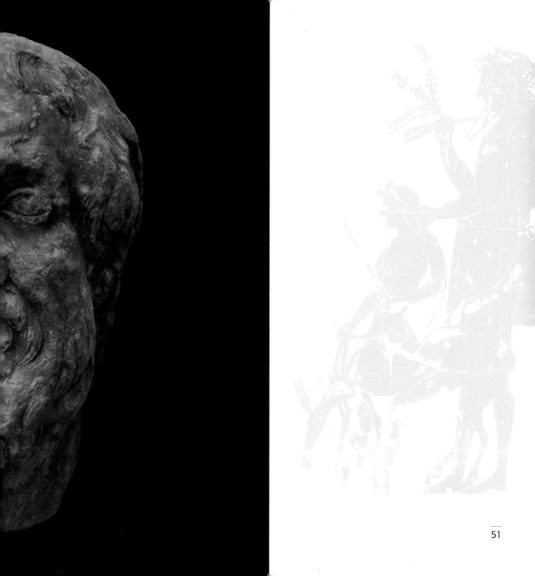

The *Iliad*

Homer's epic poem, the *Iliad*, narrates the deeds and adventures of heroic and legendary figures during the Trojan War. This riveting story has tales of bravery, love, jealousy, and betrayal.

Led by Agamemnon, the Greeks sailed a thousand ships to Troy, a city in Asia Minor (Turkey), where the beautiful Helen was held captive by the Trojan prince, Paris. After laying siege to the city for ten years, the Greeks presented Troy with an unexpected gift: a giant wooden horse with Greek soldiers hidden inside. The horse was hauled into the city, sealing Troy's fate.

Achilles Avenging Patroclos

Hector, leader of the Trojan army, mistakenly killed Patroclos, thinking he was Achilles. Blind with rage at the death of his friend, Achilles killed Hector, tied his body to a chariot, and dragged it around Patroclos' tomb.

The *Odyssey*

Picking up where the *Iliad* left off, Homer's epic poem the *Odyssey* describes the ten-year long return voyage of the Greek hero Odysseus from Troy to his wife and son in Ithaca. Odysseus had offended Poseidon, god of the sea, and the journey home was fraught with peril. Gifted as he was with both courage and intelligence, he eventually overcame all obstacles and returned home.

Fragment of a Krater (Vase)
Clay
Argos, around 670 BCE

The Blinding of Polyphemus

Odysseus and his men blinded
Polyphemus, the man-eating Cyclops,
by piercing his single eye.

Geometric Period

Geometric vases were monumental
grave markers introduced during the
Geometric period. Geometric pottery
decoration is characterized by repeated
stylized motifs, such as the meander.
Scenes illustrating the daily lives of
the aristocratic class also began to
appear. These included funerary rituals:
the dead ceremoniously displayed on
funerary pyres, funerary processions,
and funerary games held in honour of
the deceased.

Amphora

When chariot races appear on funerary
vases such as this, they are generally
associated with games held in honour
of the deceased. Some of the rituals
developed by the emerging aristocracy
— seeking to demonstrate their
power and social position — recall the
ceremonies described by Homer.

Warrior's Funeral Pyre
Eleutherna, 750–700 BCE

A Homeric Warrior's Funeral Pyre

In the *Iliad*, Homer described the funeral of Patroclos, Achilles' closest friend, who was killed at Troy. In addition to the traditional cremation of Patroclos's body on a funeral pyre, 12 Trojan soldiers were decapitated to avenge his death.

At Eleutherna on Crete, archaeologists discovered the remains of a funeral pyre from the 8th century BCE, containing the charred remains of an illustrious warrior and his companion, with a decapitated skeleton lying nearby.

The warrior would have been placed on a funeral pyre — as would his companion — allowing his soul to travel on the flames to the underworld. This warrior was found with his weapons, funerary vessels and, resting near his knees, the head of a captive — condemned, without the rest of his body, to remain trapped between the world of the living and the dead.

The Lady from Aigai
Cemetery at Aigai,
9th century BCE

The Lady from Aigai

This burial of an aristocratic woman from the ancient city of Aigai in Macedon suggests that various influences — in this case Greek and Thracian — existed side by side in the period that followed the fall of Mycenae.

Aristocrats and Warriors of Archaic Greece

7th to 6th Centuries BCE

Archaic Greece was a time of prosperity and expansion. Greek colonies spread across the Mediterranean world, bringing Greek language and culture with them. The city-state was a newly developed microcosm of the Greek world. Built around temples and trade, these city-states saw the free exchange of people, ideas and goods, a perfect mix for artistic expression to flourish.

N

Adriatic
Sea

Archontiko ○○ Sindos

Ionian Sea

Aegean Sea

Thebes ─ ○

Argos ─ ○

○ Athens

○ Samos

○ Delos

Sea of Crete

Mediterranean Sea

The Tomb of the Lady of Archontiko
Pella, Archontiko,
around 540–530 BCE

The Lady of Archontiko

Around 540 BCE, the wife of a Bottiaean ruler, dressed in her best gown and adorned with fine jewellery, was buried in the cemetery at Archontiko. The gold mask covering her face, and other objects found in her grave, indicate her status as the pride of her *oikos* (house), and her identity as a high priestess. She was the incarnation and mediator of divine blessing for the community.

More than 1,000 graves were discovered in the ancient cemetery of the Bottiaean city near the modern village of Archontiko (northwest of Pella). The Lady of Archontiko was buried in an elite section of the cemetery, in the same area as some of the warriors presented next.

Helmets
Bronze, gold
Archontiko, after 530 BCE

Expressions of Power

Whether warriors or not, the wealthy and powerful men of Archaic Greece wore helmets and carried swords and shields. This justified their status and displayed their power, even in the grave. These helmets were never used, given that there are no signs of wear. They were not meant for fighting, but to indicate the deceased's rank in the Underworld.

Kouroi and Korai

In the 7th and 6th centuries BCE, statues of young men (*kouros*; *kouroi* plural) and young women (*kore*; *korai* plural) were placed in sanctuaries as offerings to the gods, or served as grave markers for mortals.

The male figures are always naked, although some wear belts. The female figures wear *chitons* (tunics) and *himatia* (dresses) that were once painted with vibrant colours.

Votive Kore
Parian marble, bronze
Athens, 520–510 BCE

Votive Kore

This kore, which probably held an offering to Athena in her right hand, stood on the Athenian Acropolis, in a temple dedicated to the goddess Athena. The original colours can still be seen in several areas, including the brown hair and the predominantly blue and red garments. Her diadem was probably adorned with rays of gilded bronze: a way of preventing birds from perching on the statue's head.

Geochemical analysis has allowed for a digital reconstruction of how this kore was originally painted.

Votive Kouros

This is a beautiful example of the statues created during the Late Archaic Period. It stood in the sanctuary of Apollo at the top of Mount Ptoon. The donor's dedication is recorded on the figure's thighs.

His posture is typical of a kouros. If the statue were intact, the young man's arms would be hanging by his sides, and his left leg would be thrust forward, as though he were walking. This dynamic pose would help balance the heavy mass.

Votive Kouros
Parian marble
Mount Ptoon, Boeotia,
around 500 BCE

Votive Kouros

This statue was discovered in a sanctuary of Apollo. Everything about this young man catches the eye: his slender, harmonious proportions; a meticulous hairstyle that contrasts with the smooth skin; and a wide, gentle smile that adds to his noble grace. This magnificent work from central Greece was strongly influenced by styles from the Aegean islands.

Votive Kouros
Off-white Boeotian marble
Mount Ptoon, Boeotia,
mid-6th century BCE

Athletes and Citizens of Classical Greece

5th to 4th Centuries BCE

During the Classical Period, more than a thousand city-states shared an uneasy coexistence. Pan-Hellenic games — to which the entire Greek world was invited — would briefly interrupt the conflict.

Despite ongoing tensions, philosophy, theatre and rhetoric flourished, particularly in Athens, which would ultimately give humankind a precious gift: democracy.

The Birth of the Olympic Games

In 776 BCE, during the Archaic Period, athletes converged on Olympia to take part in the world's first Olympic Games, a tradition that continued in Greece for more than a thousand years.

Every four years, for several days, city-states sent their best athletes to compete with one another on the field, helping to re-establish political ties in a common celebration.

In addition to the Olympic Games, three other Pan-Hellenic games were held every two or four years: the Pythian Games in Delphi; the Nemean Games in Nemea; and the Isthmian Games in Corinth. Though athletic competitions were the main attraction, the arts were not neglected, either: in Athens, the Panathenaic Games also featured contests in poetry, music, song and dance.

Honouring Herakles

In some accounts, Herakles is credited with founding the Olympic Games. This heroic figure, son of a mortal woman and Zeus, father of the gods, is also known for undertaking twelve "labours." The word "athlete" comes from the Greek word *athlos* (labour).

Greek athletes trained and competed in the nude, but first they rubbed olive oil from an *aryballos* into their skin. After exercise, athletes ran a *strigil* over their skin to remove the sweat, sand and oil.

Aryballos (Oil Jug)
Clay
500-490 BCE
Provenance unknown, first quarter of the 5th century BCE

Strigil
Bronze
Eretria, 5th to 4th centuries BCE

Kylix Featuring Herakles

Herakles wrestled with the giant Antaios, who gained strength each time he touched the ground, thanks to his mother, Gaia, goddess of the Earth. Herakles, however, won the match, defeating his opponent by lifting him and crushing him in a bear hug.

Red-Figure Kylix
Orange-red clay
500-490 BCE
Work of the Douris Painter

A Turning Point –
The Battle of Thermopylae

King Darius I of Persia attempted to invade Greece in 490 BCE. The Persians were repelled at the Battle of Marathon, but that defeat did not sit well with the Persians. Ten years later, King Xerxes set out with a massive Persian force to crush the Greeks once and for all and to avenge his father, Darius.

The stage was set. The Persians had one of the largest armies ever assembled, but many soldiers were slaves and forced to fight. The Greeks were in disarray. They were made up of a series of feuding city-states, many of whom were happy to surrender and accept Persian rule. At stake was the fledging idea of democracy.

What unfolded during three days in August 480 BCE at Thermopylae changed history and gave way to the Classical Period of Greece.

Modern scholars estimate the Persian force to be around 200,000 strong, including 10,000 of the infamous "Immortals," the elite guard of King Xerxes himself. Alongside 300 Spartan soldiers fought 7,000 Greeks from other cities.

The Persians threatened to fire so many arrows that they would block out the sun. Undaunted, the Spartans proclaimed that they would then have their fight in the shade.

After two days of repelling all Persian advances, the Greeks were betrayed by one of their own, Ephialtes, who told the Persians of a secret goat path through the mountains. The Greeks were surrounded and all those who remained perished.

The Spartan defeat gave hope to the Greeks that the massive force of Xerxes could be beaten. After a Greek naval victory at Salamis and the final decisive battle at Plataea, the Persian War had been won. The courage and sacrifice of a few allowed Western Civilization to develop.

Statue of a Hoplite
Known as 'Leonidas'
Parian marble
Spartan Acropolis, 480-470 BCE

Athens –
An Enduring Legacy

During the Classical Period, citizens of Athens challenged conventional wisdom and presented the Western World with philosophy, theatre, science, medicine and art.

Athens was also the birthplace of democracy. For the first time, citizens were able to express themselves, debate issues and vote.

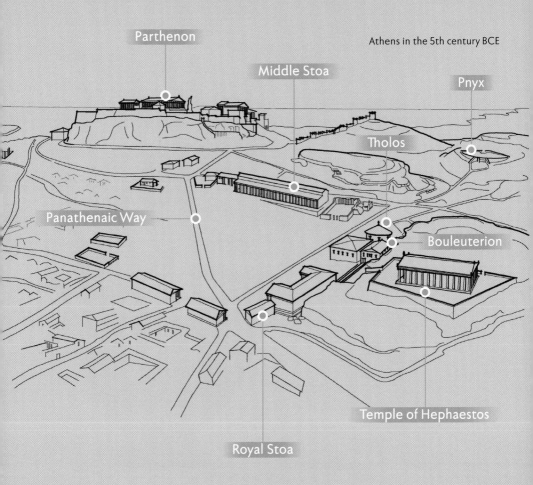

Parthenon

Middle Stoa

Athens in the 5th century BCE

Pnyx

Tholos

Bouleuterion

Panathenaic Way

Temple of Hephaestos

Royal Stoa

The Contest Between Athena and Poseidon

Athena and Poseidon presented the Athenians with lavish gifts, each hoping to become patron god of the city. The goddess planted a seed that grew into an olive tree. The god of the sea struck a blow with his trident, creating a saltwater spring. The goddess won the contest, and the city was called Athens in her honour.

Red-Figure Hydria
Clay, decorated by
the Pronomos Painter
Athens, late 5th to
early 4th centuries BCE

The Ten Tribes of Athens

**Scale model of the
Monument of the
Eponymous Heroes**
Plaster
Athens, modern replica,
second half of the 4th century BCE

Bronze statues of the ten mythical
heroes who protected Athens
once stood in the Agora. Each hero
represented an Athenian tribe. Citizens
of all trades, social classes and regions
were equally distributed among these
tribes, in order to avoid partisan politics.
The ten groups formed the basic
structure of the Athenian government.

This monument, which was 15 meters
wide, was located at the heart of
Athenian democracy, where public
notices were displayed.

A Metaphor for Democracy – Youth Crowning Himself

This sculpture may have been offered in gratitude by an athlete following a victory, possibly in the pentathlon or a naval contest. It shows a young athlete placing an olive wreath on his head, or perhaps preparing to dedicate it to the goddess Athena.

This image has become a symbol of Athenian democracy, which arose during the 5th century BCE. From now on, people would no longer be subject to the will of the gods, but instead be masters of their own fate.

Votive Bas-Relief of the Youth Crowning Himself
Parian marble
Sounion, around 460 BCE

The Tools of Democracy

The citizens of Athens had the right to vote and were expected to perform certain civic duties in return. These tools are associated with some of those duties.

Klepsydra
Clay
Athens,
5th century BCE

Kleroterion (Allotment Machine)

Kleroterion (Allotment Machine)
Pentelic marble
Hadrian's Gymnasium, 162–161 BCE

A *kleroterion* allowed the random selection of jurors and other officials. Along the front of the machine — simplified in the depiction on this object — were columns of slots representing the Athenian tribes. The names of each potential juror, inscribed on bronze plaques called *pinakia*, were placed in the slots. A number of black and white balls was released to randomly select the jurors. A white ball indicated that all jurors in a horizontal row had been chosen to serve, while a black ball meant they had all been dismissed.

Klepsydra

A water clock like this was used to set a time limit for speeches during trials. With a speaker's first words, the stopper at the base of the upper vessel was removed, and water began filling the lower vessel. Experienced speakers kept an eye on the device and concluded their remarks just as their time literally ran out. This *klepsydra* would have allowed a speech lasting six minutes.

Juror's Ballots

Once the plaintiff and defendant had finished presenting their cases, each juror was asked to vote on a verdict.

If a jury member thought the defendant's case was solid, they voted by placing a solid ballot in the voting urn, and the pierced ballot in the discard urn.

If, however, a jury member thought the defendant's case was full of holes, he placed the pierced ballot in the voting urn and the solid ballot in the other.

Jurors were careful to hold the ballot by the middle to ensure that no one could see how they had voted.

**Ostrakon of Aristeides,
Son of Lysimachos**
Clay
Athens, ostracized in 482 BCE

**Ostraka of Themistokles,
Son of Neokles**
Clay
Athens, 480s BCE (ostracized in 472 BCE)

Forced into Exile

To limit excessive political power, Athens developed the practice of ostracism. Each year, the Citizens' Assembly would first vote on whether or not to hold an ostracism. If they voted yes, they returned two months later, casting a secret vote by incising the name of the person they wished to exile on a fragment of pottery (*ostrakon*; *ostraka*, plural). The person chosen by the majority was then exiled for a period of ten years, without a trial. Only twelve Athenians were ever known to have been ostracized.

Ostrakon of Aristeides, Son of Lysimachos

Aristeides "the Just" earned his moniker when an illiterate man asked him to write on an ostrakon for him. "What name shall I write?" he asked. "Aristeides," the man answered. True to his word, Aristeides wrote his own name.

Ostraka of Themistokles, Son of Neokles

An ardent democrat, Themistokles saved Greece by convincing Athenians to use the profits from their silver mines to build ships, instead of frittering away the money. Less than a decade after leading the Athenian navy to victory at the Battle of Salamis, however, he was ostracized. Athenians were exasperated by his arrogance and ambition. Even the savior of Athens could not escape the democratic will.

Theatre in Classical Greece

Early festivals of Dionysus, god of wine, always featured public recitations. From these festivals, a tradition of performance and theatre was born, developing into two main genres. The first was tragedy, in which the story began well but finished poorly for the protagonist, a genre at which Sophocles excelled. The second was comedy, in which the story began badly but finished well.

Onstage, actors wore clay masks like the marble ones displayed here, which once adorned public buildings.

Tragedy Mask
Pentelic marble
Athens, 1st century BCE

Tragedy Mask
Pentelic marble
Attica, 3rd century BCE

Philosophy

In the thoughts and writings that they shared with their contemporaries and which ultimately spread throughout the world, Greek philosophers probed the human soul with a profundity that remains as relevant today as ever.

Plato, the Theorist (428/427 – 348/347 BCE)

A student of Socrates and teacher of Aristotle, Plato founded the Academy in Athens, the first school of higher learning in the ancient world. His *Republic* laid the foundation for western philosophy and science.

Head of Plato
Pentelic marble
Athens, Roman copy of an
original dating to about 360 BCE

**Double-Faced Portrait
of Aristotle from a Herm**
Pentelic marble
Athens, Roman copy of an original dating
to the last quarter of the 4th century BCE

Aristotle, the Observer (384–322 BCE)

Aristotle, one of the world's first scientists, embraced the study of the world around him with scientific methods based on observation. One side of this bust shows him as a young man and the other, as a wise old man.

Aristotle also tutored the young Alexander the Great.

**Portrait of the
Orator Demosthenes**
Pentelic marble
Athens, 2nd century CE Roman copy
of a Greek original dating to 280 BCE

Demosthenes, the Orator (384–322 BCE)

Demosthenes is considered the greatest Greek orator. Sixty of his speeches have survived. He was a fervent supporter of Athenian democracy and stressed the need to oppose Philip II of Macedon in his war against Athens.

Lekythos Depicting Women Caring for a Small Boy
Clay, decorated by the Painter of Bologna 228
Eretria, 470–460 BCE

Hydria Depicting a Bride and Her Friends
Clay, decorated by the Peleus Painter
Markopoulo, around 430 BCE

White-Ground Lekythos
Clay, decorated by the Achilles Painter
Eretria, 445–435 BCE

Funerary Pottery

These *lekythoi* and *hydria*, recovered from graves near Athens, depict daily life in Classical Greece and the rituals associated with death. They carry scenes of child rearing, marriages and funerals.

Votive Relief Offered to Asklepios

In the centre of this relief, Asklepios, god of medicine, leans on his staff, around which a snake is coiled. This symbol still represents medicine today.

Accompanied on the right by his children, he receives the tributes of mortals (smaller in size) whom he has cured. This type of object was placed in sanctuaries dedicated to the god.

Asklepios learned, to his folly, that even a god cannot cheat the rules of life and death. He had used the blood of a Gorgon to bring a man back from the dead. But Hades, god of the Underworld, complained to Zeus, who struck Asklepios dead with a lightning bolt. Even gods must respect life and death.

Votive Relief
Pentelic marble
Loukou, 375–350 BCE

Kings of Ancient Macedon

4th Century BCE

In the first half of the 4th century BCE, the Kingdom of Macedon emerged from the crippling strife that plagued much of Greece. The young King Philip II proved a more than capable leader. He would unify Greece through a series of military victories and strategic alliances. Philip's son, Alexander the Great, would go even further. Conquering a large portion of the ancient world, he was seen as a god, and would be immortalized for all time.

Greece Under Philip II

Adriatic Sea

Pella

Amphipolis

Aigai

Chaeronea

Aegean Sea

Ionian Sea

Mediterranean Sea

Sea of Crete

Macedonian Elites and Death

In Macedon, ritual and religion were of paramount importance. When a member of the aristocratic class, called the *hetairoi* (royal companions), died, family members made lavish preparations to ensure the comfort of the deceased in the afterlife. They also saw to the body's cremation, perpetuating the funeral rites described by Homer for their illustrious ancestors.

Contemporaries believed that, at death, a person's soul descended into the Underworld. After paying Charon, the ferryman, for passage, it travelled the River Styx to the land of the dead. A stop at the cave of Hypnos made the soul forget life on Earth.

Grave Stele

Stelae such as this marked the graves of ordinary citizens.

Two typical Macedonian names are inscribed on this one: Xenokratis, son of Pierionos and Drykalos, son of Pierionos, who were likely brothers. They confirm what Hesiod and Herodotus both state: that the Macedonians were closely related to the Magnetes of Thessaly and the Dorians of southern Greece.

Grave Stele
Marble
Aigai, 4th century BCE

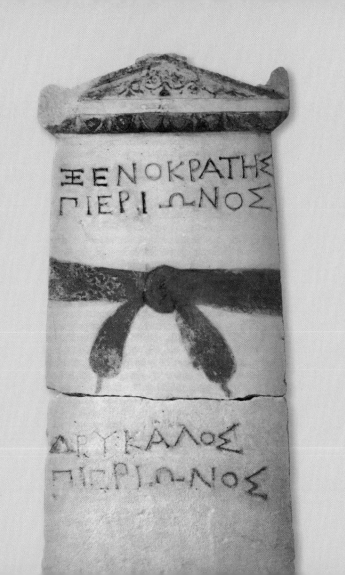

ΞΕΝΟΚΡΑΤΗΣ
ΠΙΕΡΙΩΝΟΣ

ΔΡΥΚΑΛΟΣ
ΠΙΕΡΙΩΝΟΣ

The Abduction of Persephone Fresco

In the Kingdom of the Dead

Persephone, daughter of Zeus and Demeter, was goddess of the harvest. She was abducted by Hades, god of the Underworld, who made her his queen. Seeing Demeter's despair at the loss of her daughter, Zeus decided that Persephone would return to earth each spring, which allowed grain to sprout and feed humanity. Persephone thus became a symbol of immortality and the seasons.

Initiates into the Eleusinian Mysteries — rituals performed at Eleusis — believed that Persephone had the power to preserve human memory. They asked her to help them remember their lives when it was time make their own way to the kingdom of the dead.

Gold Leaf
Gold
Pella, late 4th century BCE

Leaf Bearing the Name of a Devotee of the Eleusinian Mysteries

The name of a woman — ΓΙΣΙΣΚΑ (Hegesiska) — who was an initiate into mystic rites is engraved on this gold myrtle leaf, an afterlife symbol for the devotee as she was presenting herself before the goddess Persephone, Queen of the Underworld.

Myrtle Wreath
Gold, enamel
350–325 BCE

Gold Myrtle Wreath

Although it has lost some of its flowers, this golden wreath features two incredibly lifelike branches of myrtle, an aromatic plant associated with the beautiful Aphrodite and a symbol of immortality. In Macedon, similar objects have been found in the graves of wealthy men and women. Wreaths of gold, gilded or made of natural materials, were worn during public or secret rituals, and at symposia, games, theatrical performances, and other events.

The Priestly Warrior of Stavroupolis

In 1974, a small stone tomb was unearthed during construction work in Stavroupolis, Thessaloniki. Archaeologists determined that the man buried there had likely been cremated. A wooden box containing ritual vessels, a writing case, and weapons painted a clearer picture of him. He was a scholar, probably a priest, a warrior, and a member of the aristocratic *hetairoi*, royal companions to the king of Macedon.

He may have spent part of his youth as one of the boys allowed to accompany the king on a hunt, making him familiar with the weapons that would allow him to kill an animal — or an enemy. Along with physical training and learning to read and write, this formed a boy's passage into adulthood.

Kleita, Priestess of Derveni

In Macedonian society, when a girl turned 14, she was usually expected to marry a man chosen for her, and to provide him with legitimate heirs. She was also required to oversee the smooth running of her household, applying what she had been taught by older women since childhood. In addition, she would take part in festivals honouring Demeter and her daughter, Persephone, or the cult of Dionysos.

The rich objects found in the tomb of a Macedonian woman paint a more personal portrait. A ring reveals her name: Kleita. A pendant shaped like the head of Herakles, found at her neck, suggests that she was a member of the *hetairoi*: companions of the royal family claiming descent from the hero himself. She was clearly a high-ranking noblewoman, head of a large household comprised of slaves and servants. She may even have been a priestess, or a powerful healer.

Gold Amulet Pendant

This gold pendant is in the shape of the head of Herakles. The pendant is forged from a thick sheet. The figure's eyelashes and mustache and the fur of the lion's skin are incised.

Herakles was the mythical ancestor of the Temenid dynasty, and members of Macedon's aristocratic families may have worn such pendants to make their family connections known.

Philip II, the King Who Unified Greece

Philip II, King of Macedon, was a man of genius — an excellent strategist, a skilled diplomat and surely one of the most capable statesmen of all times. He accomplished something no one had ever done before, with the exception of the mythical King Agamemnon: the unification of Greece.

Amulet Pendant
Gold
Derveni, Tomb Z, 300-280 BCE

Oinochoe (Wine Jug)
Silver

Greaves (Leg Guards)
Bronze

Diadem
Silver, gold

Gorgon Head
Gold

Philip II's Tomb, Aigai, 336 BCE

Oinochoe

This silver *oinochoe* is decorated with a relief head of the satyr, Silenus, a mythical figure associated with Dionysus, the god of wine. It is one of the finest surviving examples in the Greek world.

Diadem

This priceless silver and gold diadem, perhaps worn by Philip II at the time of his assassination, symbolized his supreme political, military and religious authority. Note the metal "Herakles Knot," imitating a cloth headband. The knot was a reminder that the Macedonian king was a direct descendant of the Greek hero and his father Zeus, father of the gods.

Greaves

These greaves, a common form of body armour in the period, were tailored to fit the shins of Philip II. Philip had suffered a broken tibia when his horse fell on him in battle, leaving one leg misshapen.

Gorgon Head

This is one of two Gorgon heads that adorned Philip II's linen and leather cuirass. It is one of the earliest and probably the most important surviving example of this type of adornment. Very popular in ancient times, this ornament was thought to offer protection from evil. According to legend, anyone who looked in the eyes of a snake-haired Gorgon turned to stone.

In 336 BCE, Alexander the Great buried his father Philip II. He did so in grand fashion with an elaborate tomb and all the trappings of a Homeric hero. Alexander used the occasion to stake his claim on the empire his father had built. On his father's tomb, Alexander had himself painted at the centre, leaving no doubt who was now king of Macedon.

Tomb Facade of Philip II
Philip's Tomb, Aigai, 336 BCE

Meda, 6th Wife of Philip II

This gold wreath, worn by Queen
Meda, is one of the most remarkable
gold objects of the ancient world.
With hundreds of leaves and blossoms,
the myrtle is remarkably realistic
and graceful.

Philip II had seven wives, but Meda, a
Thracian princess, was the only one
who had the privilege of being buried
in his tomb. As was the custom in
Thrace, she threw herself on his funeral
pyre in order to follow him to the
Kingdom of the Dead.

Gold Myrtle Crown
Gold
Aigai, antechamber of the
Tomb of Philip II, 336 BCE

Alexander the Great
(356–323 BCE)

Sculpted shortly after Alexander's death, this bust depicts him in the flower of youth.

Several portraits were produced of Alexander — both during his lifetime and after his death — by important painters and sculptors. In this depiction, a number of details, supported by rare physical descriptions of Alexander from ancient writings, make it possible to recognize him: the slight tilt of his head, the arrangement of his hair, his lack of beard, unusual for kings in this period, and his upward glance. The rendering of his hair, his slightly opened mouth, and the working of the marble result in a portrait that is both realistic and idealized.

For many years after Alexander's death, his image was used by successors who sought to associate themselves with his legend.

Bust of Alexander the Great
Marble
Pella, end of the 4th century BCE

Statue of Alexander as Pan

Alexander the Great is portrayed here with the horns and tail of Pan, god of the wilderness. Although he was not the first Greek king to claim a divine nature, the ancient world adopted and maintained the legend of Alexander's divinity for centuries to come.

Alexander as Pan
Marble
Pella, late 4th or
early 3rd century BCE

A New World –
The Hellenistic Age

After 323 BCE

**Tetradrachm
of Lysimachus**
Silver
Provenance unknown,
297/296 – 282/281 BCE

Building on a strong foundation from Philip II, Alexander the Great conquered much of the known world, becoming the King of Macedon, Pharoah of Egypt, King of Persia and King of Asia. In his short life, he united East and West, spreading the ideas of the Classical Greek world and adopting many local customs and traditions. Not without flaws, he was quick to anger, stubborn and overconfident, and most certainly mortal: Alexander would succumb to a fever in 323 BCE in Babylon. Even after his death, Alexander's legend continued to grow and he inspired leaders from Julius Caesar to Napoleon.

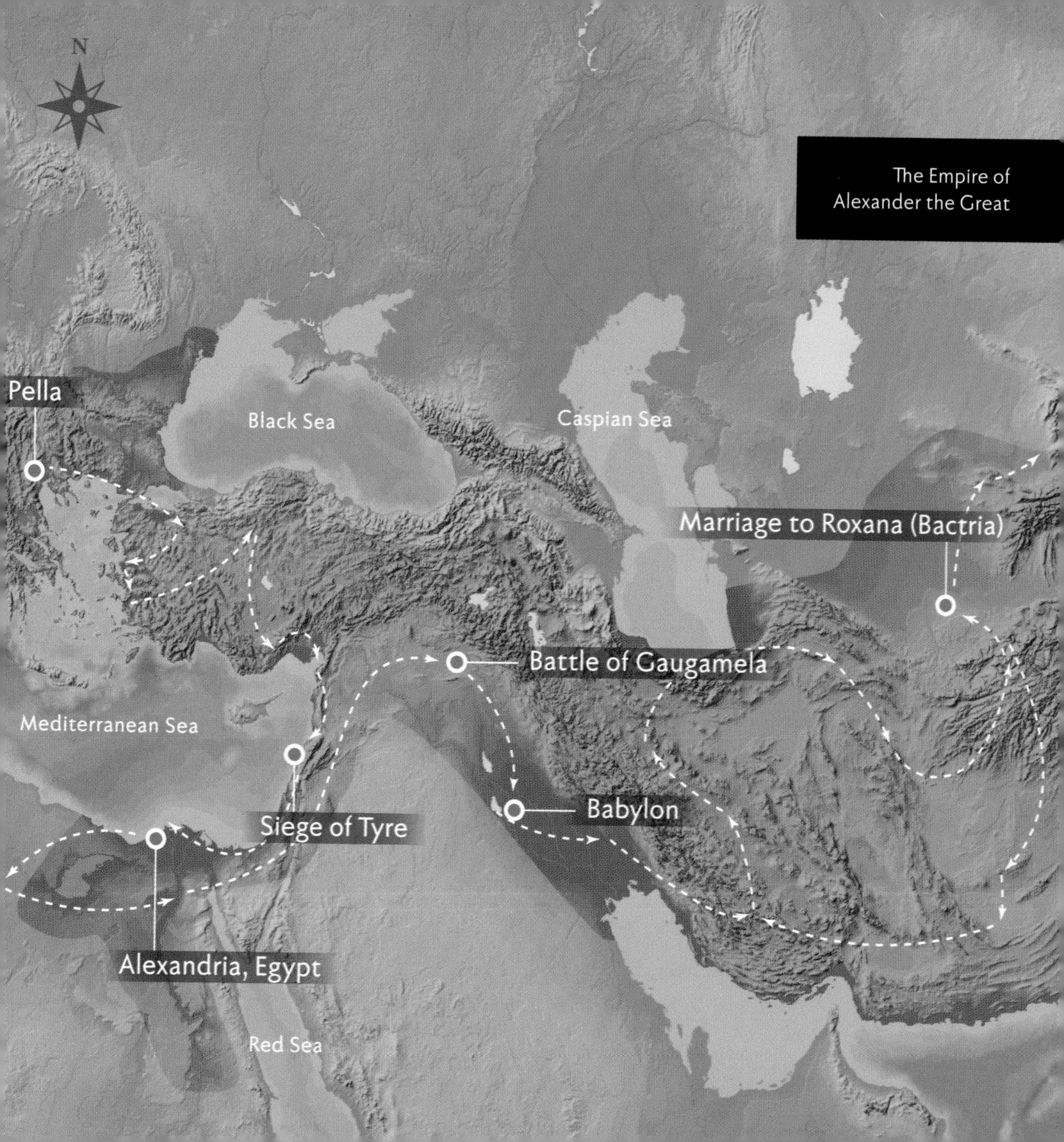

The Empire of Alexander the Great

Pella

Black Sea

Caspian Sea

Marriage to Roxana (Bactria)

Battle of Gaugamela

Mediterranean Sea

Siege of Tyre

Babylon

Alexandria, Egypt

Red Sea

Contributions

I wish to acknowledge the contribution of the scientific and creative team: Jean-François Léger, William Parkinson, Fredrik Hiebert, and Jacques Perreault. A heartfelt thanks to our Greek colleagues, most notably Maria Vlazaki, Anastasia Balaska and the entire Greek Scientific Committee. From the Canadian Museum of History: Cathy Mitchell, Danièle Goulet, Kerri Davis, Rick Rocheleau, Patrice Rémillard, Nadine Marsolais, Stéphane Breton, Frank Wimart and Jean-Marc Blais, merci beaucoup. Thank you to our text team of Annick Poussart, Sheila Singhal and Paula Sousa. From the consortium: Kathryn Keane, Gretchen Baker, Jaap Hoogstraten and Christine Dufresne. My sincerest thanks to Stavros Niarchos New Media Lab, Andre Gerolymatos and Costa Dedigakas. Thank you to H.E. Eleftherios Anghelopoulos, H.E. Robert Peck, and Athanasia Papatriantafyllou. Our research team of Leah Iselmoe, Sabrina Higgins, Amber Polywkan, and the University of Ottawa Museum of Classical Antiquities were invaluable. To the entire myriad others who contributed to this amazing project, thank you.

Sas efkaristo!

Photo Credits